Disney ALICE IN WONDERLAND

Level 5

Re-told by: Mary Tomalin
Series Editor: Rachel Wilson

Contents

In This Book

Alice

A young woman trying to find out who she is

Hamish

A rich, young man who wants to marry Alice

Stayne

The Knave of Hearts, a soldier who works for the Red Queen and is her friend

The Red Queen

A queen who rules Underland and frightens people

The Mad Hatter

A man who makes wonderful hats. He is funny, kind, and a little strange!

The White Queen

The Red Queen's kind and sweet younger sister

Before You Read

Introduction

Alice Kingsleigh often has a bad dream, where she falls down a rabbit hole and meets strange people and creatures. When Alice is nineteen, she *does* fall down a rabbit hole. She opens a door into a place called Underland and meets the people and creatures in her dream. But there's danger for her and everyone there. The Mad Hatter, the White Queen, and their friends need Alice's help …

Activities

1 Read *In This Book* and the *Introduction*. **What do you think will happen in this story?**

1 Alice will marry the Mad Hatter.

2 Alice will help the people of Underland.

3 Alice will fight the Red Queen.

4 Alice will fight the White Queen.

2 Use the *Glossary* to find the meaning of the words in bold. Then match the two parts of the sentences.

1 The **huge creature**

2 The men **attacked** the castle

3 A girl suddenly **appeared**

4 She **recognized**

5 Strange things happen in dreams

a her friend.

b and made a **hole** in the walls.

c but they are not **real**.

d started running toward her.

e at a window.

1 It's Only a Dream

It was night-time, and nine-year-old Alice Kingsleigh suddenly
woke up. She felt very scared. Her father came and sat by her bed.

"The bad dream again?" he asked.

"Yes!" said Alice. "I'm falling down a dark hole, then I see
strange creatures. There's a rabbit in a coat, a cat that can smile,
and a blue caterpillar."

"A blue caterpillar!" said her father, and smiled. "It's only a
dream, Alice. Nothing can hurt you there."

2 Down the Rabbit Hole

When Alice was nineteen, she went to a garden party with her mother. Her father was dead now.

Alice still had long, fair hair. She still had the same bad dream and she liked thinking about strange things. She felt different than other people.

She danced with Hamish, a rich, young man who was very boring.

"Do you ever think you would like to fly?" she asked him.

"Why think about things which are not possible? Meet me over there in ten minutes," Hamish said, and pointed.

Hamish left her, and two friends came to talk to her.

"Hamish wants to marry you. He's going to ask you," they said.

Alice's sister pulled Alice away. "It was a surprise!" she said.

"I don't know if I want to marry Hamish …" said Alice.

Suddenly, she saw a big, white rabbit in a blue coat. She couldn't believe it—a rabbit in a coat! She followed it but couldn't find it. Then Hamish found her.

"Alice Kingsleigh, will you be my wife?" he said.

"What shall I say?" thought Alice. "I ..." she said.

Then she saw the rabbit again. She turned and ran. She followed the rabbit across a field into a wood. It ran behind a tree that had a big rabbit hole next to it. Alice looked down the hole—and fell into it. She fell for a long, long time before she hit the ground.

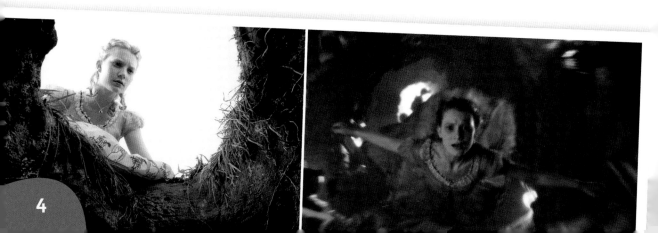

Alice stood up. She was in a round room with four doors, but she couldn't open them. She found a key on a table that opened another, very small, door. But she could only get her head through it.

Alice closed the door and put the key back on the table. But now, there was a bottle on the table with the words *Drink me* on it. So, she drank from the bottle, and suddenly she became really small.

Now Alice could go through the little door. But the key was on the table, and she was too small—she couldn't get it.

She saw a glass box on the floor. There was a cake with the words *Eat Me* on it. She ate some cake, and now she grew very tall.

"Wonderful!" Alice thought.

She took the key from the table, then drank from the bottle.

When she grew small again, she opened the door with the key.

3 A Very Strange Place

Alice was in a place called Underland. It had strange creatures and plants. After a short time, she met the White Rabbit, the Dormouse, and two twin boys.

"Who are you?" asked Alice.

"I'm Tweedledee, he's Tweedledum," said one of the boys. They took Alice to see Absolem, a big, blue caterpillar.

"Who are YOU?" he asked.

"Alice," said Alice.

"We shall see ..." said Absolem.

They opened an old, long piece of paper that was called the Oraculum. It showed the things that happened each day and all the future days, too.

"Show her the Frabjous Day," said Absolem.

"On Frabjous Day," explained Tweedledee, "you destroy the Jabberwocky."

"What?" said Alice.

She looked at the picture on the Oraculum. It moved and showed Alice in armor. She had a sword and was in a fight with a huge, frightening creature.

"That's you, there, with the Vorpal Sword," said Tweedledum.

"Only the Vorpal Sword can destroy the Jabberwocky," said Tweedledee.

"That's not me," said Alice.

"Is she the right Alice, Absolem?" the White Rabbit asked.

"Not really," said the caterpillar.

"I'm sorry!" cried Alice. "But this is *my* dream. I'm going to wake up now, and you'll all disappear." But she didn't wake up, and the creatures just looked at her.

Suddenly, a huge animal that looked like a dangerous dog appeared. "Bandersnatch!" shouted Tweedledee.

There were soldiers with the Bandersnatch—they looked like red cards. The creatures started running, and Alice ran with them. She felt very scared. Then she stopped and said, "It's only a dream," and turned to look at the Bandersnatch. The creature opened its mouth to eat her.

"Run, Alice!" shouted the Dormouse.

The Dormouse jumped on the Bandersnatch's head and put a pin in its left eye. The eye came out, and she ran away with it. Alice started running again.

In the forest, a tall soldier found the Oraculum. He was the Knave of Hearts, and his name was Stayne. He took the Oraculum to a castle—the home of the Red Queen. The Red Queen had a huge head. She was a horrible queen who liked to shout.

Stayne showed the Red Queen the picture of Alice and the Jabberwocky.

"Is it Alice?" asked the Queen.

"Yes, and she's going to destroy the Jabberwocky," said Stayne.

"Destroy my Jabberwocky?" shouted the Red Queen. "Find Alice!"

4 The Mad Hatter

Alice met the Cheshire Cat. The Cheshire Cat had a big smile and could disappear. Sometimes he just had a head! He took her to a strange house. There was a table with all the things for a tea party, and at the table were the Mad Hatter, the March Hare, and the Dormouse.

When the Mad Hatter saw Alice, he got very excited. He ran across the top of the table.

"It's you!" he shouted happily. "You're very late, you know!"

Suddenly, Stayne and his soldiers appeared. Quickly, the Mad Hatter gave Alice a drink from a bottle. She became very small, and he hid her.

"We're looking for Alice," Stayne said. But he couldn't find her and left angrily.

"Take Alice to the White Queen," said the March Hare.

The Mad Hatter put Alice on his shoulder, and they started walking through the forest. He sang a song about destroying the Jabberwocky.

"It's all about you, you know," he said.

"I'm not destroying anything!" Alice said.

"You're not the same as you were before," the Mad Hatter said angrily.

He told Alice a terrible story. The Mad Hatter made hats for the White Queen. Then one day, the White Queen's sister used the Jabberwocky to hurt people at her court. It breathed fire and destroyed his whole family. Stayne took the Vorpal Sword, and the White Queen's sister became the Queen—the Red Queen.

The Mad Hatter looked very sad and Alice felt really sorry for him.

Suddenly, they heard Stayne's soldiers. The Mad Hatter started running, but the soldiers were close. He put Alice on his hat and threw it far away.

"Down with the Red Queen!" he shouted. The soldiers took him away.

The hat flew a long way before it fell on the ground. It was night-time and Alice slept under the hat. When she woke, there was a dog there. His name was Bayard, and he didn't like the Red Queen.

5 Two Castles

"The Hatter is at the Red Queen's castle," Bayard said.

"We're going to save him!" Alice cried and rode on Bayard to the castle. She climbed through a hole in the wall and into the gardens. There, she met the White Rabbit again, and he gave her some cake. When she ate it she grew really tall.

The Red Queen found Alice. But she didn't recognize her because Alice was so tall.

"Any girl with a head *that* large is welcome in my court ..." the Queen said.

In the castle, the White Rabbit took Alice to find the Vorpal Sword. But the Bandersnatch was there, too.

"Oh, no!" thought Alice, but then she had an idea. The Dormouse was in the castle. Alice found her and got the Bandersnatch's eye from her. Then she went back to the room and gave the Bandersnatch his eye. He put it back in his head. When Alice picked up the Vorpal Sword he just looked at her.

Alice took the sword and found the Mad Hatter and the Dormouse. Then Stayne and his soldiers saw her.

"Run, Alice! cried the Dormouse.

"Alice! Get her!" cried Stayne.

Suddenly, the Bandersnatch appeared. It was friendly now. Alice climbed on its back, and it ran all the way to the White Queen's castle. Alice gave the White Queen the Vorpal Sword.

"The Vorpal Sword is home again," said the White Queen. She gave Alice a drink, and Alice became her usual height again.

The Red Queen was very angry when she heard about Alice. But she couldn't hurt Alice because Alice wasn't there.

"But we have the Hatter and the Dormouse ..." said Stayne.

"Off with their heads!" the Red Queen shouted.

Early the next morning, soldiers brought the Mad Hatter in front of the Red Queen and her court. But just before they could follow what the Red Queen said, the Mad Hatter's body disappeared! Strangely, the Cheshire Cat's head appeared under the hat!

Then the Mad Hatter appeared again.

"Stand up and fight! Down with Big Head!" he shouted.

"Down with Big Head!" people cried.

"Get my bird!" the Queen shouted angrily. Two minutes later, a huge, frightening bird flew down from the sky and started attacking people.

"Get the Jabberwocky ready for battle!" the Red Queen told Stayne. "We're visiting my little sister very soon!"

The Hatter, the Dormouse, and the White Rabbit ran out of the castle.

The White Queen was with her court, and Alice and her friends were with them.

"You still think this is a dream?" the Mad Hatter asked Alice and smiled.

"Well, it can't possibly be real," Alice said.

"Who will be the White Queen's champion?" shouted the White Rabbit. He opened the Oraculum at the picture of Alice and the Jabberwocky.

"It has to be Alice," Tweedledum said.

Alice felt terrible. She ran into the gardens. Then she sat down and cried.

"Crying won't help," said a voice. It was Absolem. "Alice, when you were here the first time, you called this place 'Wonderland'," he said.

"Wonderland!" said Alice, and suddenly she remembered everything about her dream. In the dream she was a little girl. Now, at last, Alice understood. "It wasn't a dream, it was all real!" she cried. "And this place is real!"

"The Jabberwocky is real, too. Remember—the Vorpal Sword will help you," said the caterpillar.

6 Frabjous Day

It was Frabjous Day, and the two sides were ready for battle. Alice, the White Queen's champion, was on the Bandersnatch. The Jabberwocky appeared. It was as big as a house, with red eyes, huge wings, and a long tail.

Alice felt very frightened, but she had her armor and the Vorpal Sword. It was not a dream, she knew that now. She walked toward the Jabberwocky, and they began to battle. Behind them, the soldiers fought, too.

The Jabberwocky hit Alice again and again, but the Vorpal Sword helped her. When the creature breathed white fire, it hit her armor.

There was a tall, very old building with no walls. Alice ran up the steps to the top. Suddenly, the Jabberwocky appeared above her. It looked huge. It brought its long neck down to attack her, but Alice jumped on its neck.

The creature threw her into the air. Alice held up the Vorpal Sword …

She came down on the Jabberwocky's neck and cut off its head
with the sword.

The head fell slowly down the steps. The Jabberwocky
was dead.

"Destroy Alice!" shouted the Red Queen.

But a soldier shouted, "We follow you no more ... Big Head!"
and dropped his sword on the ground. Then all the other soldiers
did the same.

The Red Queen was surprised and frightened. This was the
end for her—her sister was queen again.

"How shall we thank you?" asked the White Queen. She gave Alice a small bottle.

"Will this take me home?" Alice asked.

"Yes," said the Queen.

"You could stay," said the Mad Hatter sadly.

"I can't. There are things that I must do," Alice said. "I'll be back before you know it."

"You won't remember me," said the Hatter.

"Yes, I will. How could I forget?" Alice answered. The Mad Hatter whispered something in her ear …

7 Home Again

Alice could see the sky. She was near the top of the rabbit hole and she climbed out. The tree, the fields, everything was the same as before. After some time, she returned to the party. Hamish was still in the same place.

"She left me without an answer!" he told people angrily.

Then Alice appeared. Her dress was very dirty.

"What happened to you?" asked her mother.

"I fell down a hole and hit my head," answered Alice.

Alice turned to Hamish and said, "I'm sorry, Hamish, I can't marry you. You're not the right man for me."

Then she went to her mother. "It's all right, Mother," she said. "I shall do something good with my life."

She saw her two friends and laughed. "You two make me think of some funny boys I met in a dream!" The girls didn't understand. But Alice remembered her friends in Underland.

After You Read

1 Put the sentences into the correct order.

a Alice falls down a rabbit hole.

b Alice battles and destroys the Jabberwocky.

c Alice takes the Vorpal Sword.

d Alice tells Hamish, "I can't marry you."

e Alice meets the Mad Hatter at a tea party.

2 Choose the correct answers to the questions.

1 Why does Alice turn to look at the Bandersnatch?

  a Because she doesn't think the Bandersnatch is real.

  b Because she doesn't think the Bandersnatch is near.

2 Why does the Red Queen want to find Alice?

  a Because Alice is going to destroy the Jabberwocky.

  b Because Alice is a friend of the White Queen.

3 Why does Alice become the White Queen's champion?

  a Because she wants to help the Queen.

  b Because she wants to live in Underland.

3 What do you think? Why? Discuss with a friend.

1 Which two characters do you like best?

2 Which character is the most frightening?

3 Which character is the strangest?

Glossary

appear past tense **appeared** (*verb*) if something appears, you begin to see it; *Suddenly, a huge animal that looked like a dangerous dog appeared.*

armor (*noun*) clothes that are made of metal

attack past tense **attacked** (*verb*) to try to hurt; *It brought its long neck down to attack her, but Alice jumped on its neck.*

battle (*noun*) a fight between two sides or countries; *It was Frabjous Day, and the two sides were ready for battle.*

caterpillar (*noun*) an insect that becomes a butterfly

champion (*noun*) someone who fights for another person

court (*noun*) the important people who live and work with a king or queen

creature (*noun*) a large or small living thing that can move

dead (*adj.*) not living any more

down with (*idiom*) you say this when you don't like someone who has a lot of power

disappear past tense **disappeared** (*verb*) if something disappears, you can't see it; the opposite of appear; *I'm going to wake up now, and you'll all disappear.*

hole (*noun*) an empty space in something

huge (*adj.*) very big

look like past tense **looked like** (*verb*) to look nearly the same as something; *There were soldiers with the Bandersnatch—they looked like red cards.*

pin (*noun*) a small, thin piece of metal which holds things together

real (*adj.*) when something is real, you can see, touch, or hear it

recognize past tense **recognized** (*verb*) to know a person because you saw him or her before; *But she didn't recognize her because Alice was so tall.*

soldier (*noun*) a person who fights for his or her country

sword (*noun*) a long, thin, sharp piece of metal which soldiers use in battle

whisper past tense **whispered** (*verb*) to speak very quietly; *The Mad Hatter whispered something in her ear.*

Play: Fight for What's Right!

Scene 1:

Alice is putting on her armor. The White Queen is helping.

ALICE: I'm so afraid, but I must help the people of Underland!

MAD HATTER: Yes, Alice. You must destroy the Jabberwocky!

WHITE QUEEN: [gives Alice the sword] Here, take the Vorpal Sword. It's time.

Scene 2:

The battle begins. The Jabberwocky attacks and Alice fights back, again and again.

MAD HATTER: I'm so frightened for Alice, I can't watch!

WHITE QUEEN: It's all right. She's brave and she has the Vorpal Sword.

ALICE: [holding the sword over the Jabberwocky's neck] Aggh! Take that, Jabberwocky!

[She cuts off the Jabberwocky's head. It falls to

the ground.]

MAD HATTER: Hooray for Alice! She did it! She destroyed the Jabberwocky!

Scene 3:

After the battle.

WHITE QUEEN: You saved my people, Alice. Thank you.

ALICE: Yes, I did!

MAD HATTER: We have a good queen again because of you, Alice.

ALICE: Yes. And now it's time for me to go home.

Global Citizenship

Healthy and HAPPY

Haile Thomas was eight years old when her dad got sick. But her family didn't get sad—they got busy! The whole family changed the way they lived. They started to eat healthy food, and do more exercise. Then something wonderful happened—Haile's dad started to get better. That's how Haile understood the power of a healthy life.

Children can have health problems, too, if they don't eat well. In 2013—when Haile was only 13—she started the organization HAPPY. It helps young people to live happy, healthy lives. There are cooking classes, summer camps, and school programs.

Haile wrote a vegan cookbook in 2020. She talks to people in the US and other countries about her work.

How did the filmmakers create the Red Queen's "look"?

In a movie, a person's "look" is very important. Their face and clothes tell you a lot about them. The Red Queen looks very strange. This tells you about her character—she is not like other people.

How did the filmmakers create her look?

First, they drew pictures of her. This helped them with their ideas. They gave her a huge head! Then they thought about her makeup, hair, and clothes. They changed the size of Helena Bonham Carter's head in the film. It looks much bigger than her real head.

The Red Queen's Clothes

She's a queen so her clothes are very beautiful. She wears a lot of red. In some countries, red is the color of anger.

Helena Bonham Carter was the Red Queen in the movie

Helena Bonham Carter's makeup took about three hours every day.

1 She wore a big, red wig.
2 They made her forehead very high.
3 They drew very thin eyebrows.
4 They painted a red heart on her mouth.
5 They used a lot of white and blue makeup.

create (*verb*) to make
character (*noun*) the way that a person thinks, feels, and talks

Phonics

Say the sounds. Read the words.

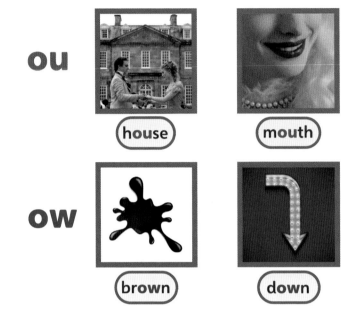

ou

house

mouth

ow

brown

down

Read, then say the rhyme to a friend.

The Mad Hatter's hat was brown and round.
When the Hatter went out, it fell on the ground.

Without a sound, that hat went down.
Then the Dormouse found it, on the ground.

"How did it fall?" the Dormouse said,
But the Hatter was out, so she went to bed.